PERFECT E-MAIL

PERFECT
E-MAIL

All you need to get it right first time

Steve Morris

RANDOM HOUSE

BUSINESS BOOKS

1 3 5 7 9 10 8 6 4 2

This edition published in the United Kingdom in 2000
by Random House Business Books

First published in 2000 by Random House Business Books,
Random House, 20 Vauxhall Bridge Road, London SW1V 2SA

Random House Australia (Pty) Limited
20 Alfred Street, Milsons Point
Sydney, New South Wales 2061, Australia

Random House New Zealand Limited
18 Poland Road, Glenfield
Auckland 10, New Zealand

Random House (Pty) Limited
Endulini, 5a Jubilee Road, Parktown 2193, South Africa

The Random House Group Limited Reg. No. 954009

Papers used by Random House are natural, recyclable
products made from wood grown in sustainable forests. The
manufacturing processes conform to the environmental regulations
of the country of origin.

ISBN 0 09 9401583 6

Companies, institutions and other organizations wishing to make
bulk purchases of any business books published by Random House
should contact their local bookstore or Random House direct:
Special Sales Director
Random House, 20 Vauxhall Bridge Road, London SW1V 2SA

Tel: 020 7840 8470 Fax: 020 7828 6681

www.randomhouse.co.uk
businessbooks@randomhouse.co.uk

Typeset in Sabon by SX Composing DTP, Rayleigh, Essex
Printed and bound in Great Britain by Cox & Wyman Ltd, Reading

Thank you

I would like to thank my colleagues Will Skidelsky and Phil Rigg. They offered me invaluable help in writing this book, drafting some sections and generally offering useful advice and inspirations. Phil added his knowledge of post-structuralism and forms of wrongness, and Will his insight into the life of Eskimos pre e-mail.

Contents

Introduction

ANYONE FOR CYBERSPACE?

A few years ago, e-mails were something that a few people, often known as cyber-geeks, knew how to use. It sounded quite exciting. But it wasn't something that was directly relevant to the lives of most normal people. While a few funny folks with long hair and glasses spent their time tapping away, in permanent communication with one another, the rest of the world made do with conventional forms of communication – the letter (diminishingly), the phone (increasingly and both fixed and mobile) and the fax – and were for the most part happy to do so.

But what a difference a few years make. These days, everyone seems to be on e-mail. If you're not on-line at home, you're probably hooked up at work. If you're not hooked up at work, you probably visit Internet cafés. If you've never been in an Internet café, well, we can only suggest you're holed up in a time capsule somewhere. Apparently a popular present to give a new-born infant is their own personal e-mail address they can keep for life. Truly the e-mail is coming of age. The real convenience of it has done much to encourage its use, until these days company's bike bills have dropped dramatically as e-mails and assorted attachments whip across cyberspace.

And with this massive change, the significance of being able to use e-mail effectively has also changed. It is no longer simply a quirky tool, reserved for the knowledgeable few. Far more than this: the skill of using it is fast becoming a pre-condition of functioning in the modern world.

Quite simply, e-mail is becoming *the* way to communicate. And it will only go on getting more important.

The pace of change

Our aim here is to consider, at different levels, the *meaning* of the e-mail and why we need to really get used to this new form of writing. So we'll look at what it means for communication generally, and also what it means for you. And there is a profound point here. Just a few years ago we were confidently told of the death of writing and the death of letters. Youngsters, and the rest of us come to that, apparently preferred talking on the telephone to sitting down and writing a letter. In business things got less stuffy, so the telephone seemed to predominate there too.

But with e-mail the call goes up:

Writing is dead, long live writing . . .

. . . because e-mail has reinvented communication by making writing sexy, fun and vital again. This natty little 'almost-letter' is relaunching the written word. Not in the sonorous, voluminous style of old. But quick, sharp and fun. In homes and offices around the world people are waking up to the power of e-mail.

Interestingly, because e-mail software is so crude at present and offers few design touches, it throws the words into sharp relief. Without the comfort of design all you notice are the simple old words. Which again brings writing to the forefront.

We will see that the challenge presented by the e-mail is primarily a matter of responding effectively to change.

Change is never a simple thing, though there are those who claim it is. As a species, our ability to adapt to it is one of the things that makes us so much more successful than other animals. But one penalty of our success in adapting is that by doing so we have given ourselves the capacity to invent new ways of doing things. And by thinking up these new ways we are forcing upon ourselves the need to adapt anew.

Up to say a hundred years ago, change was slow and the adjustments that an individual would have to make in a lifetime were minimal. Adaptation was 'invisible', being enacted over generations. This is no longer the case. Significant changes now take place in a matter of decades, even less. For instance, who'd even heard of the Internet ten years ago?

What this means, of course, is that individuals need to develop the ability to constantly change with the times. Think of all the huge changes a person now aged seventy will have seen in their lifetime. Apart from living through the monstrosities of the Second World War, they will have seen the invention of television, the nuclear bomb, mass air travel, the personal computer, the fax and mobile television and, only now, the coming of the digital and Internet revolutions.

That's a lot of change for one person to cope with!

But just think about how much more change those growing up now will see in their lifetimes.

The challenge of e-mail
This is both tremendously exciting and a massive challenge. Everyone who has experienced the thrill of

writing an e-mail will know just how exciting it really is. It holds out revolutionary new possibilities for bite-sized communication in a newly-connected world out there.

But at the same time, there is a certain amount of uncertainty, even worry, associated with the e-mail. How are we supposed to write them? After all, because of the haphazard way that e-mails have grown up there has never been any attempt to establish a set of conventions for writing them. And are many e-mails very clumsy? Just look at the faltering steps of e-mail marketers and we see a discipline, shall we say kindly, in its infancy. E-mail is still to establish a way of being and doing.

Perhaps because of this level of uncertainty, e-mails have naturally come to resemble spoken conversation much more than written letters. This in itself is one of the most refreshing things about the e-mail revolution. The pressure generated by this conversational style cannot but fail to have an impact on language in general. Though the traditionalists will no doubt try and knock the informality out of e-communication for good, we can only hope they will fail, and that the conversational benefits will remain.

But at the same time, there is urgent need now for some kind of basic conventions for writing e-mails. This is especially true at the business level, where it is becoming increasingly important to establish some consistency in the writing and handling of e-mails.

These are issues which need to be thought about and acted upon. And it is exactly this task, we hope, that this book will help with.

What this book does
In each section we'll be looking at a particular aspect of the world of electronic mail, to help you get a firm grasp of how it works at different levels. Our focus becomes

more defined as you read on; for instance, you'll get a broad sense of the business context of e-mails before getting down to the nitty-gritty of e-mail language analysis. By the end of the book you'll have a deeper insight into:

1 **Understanding e-mails** – challenges and opportunities of the new technology.
2 **Letting go of the old formulas** . . . and opening up to new ideas.
3 **Acting** – putting your learning into practice.
4 **Wrong use of language** – classic flaws in business e-mails.
5 **New principles of tone** – best practice for business e-mails.

THE THREE A'S OF ADAPTATION

To help us think about electronic mail and its effects, we'll introduce each of the A's of Adaptation here and now, then explore them at length in the three chapters that follow.

1 Appreciating

Adaptation involves appreciating the potential value of the new. Call it the vision thing if you like. In order to adapt, you must be able to see the possibilities inherent in new inventions and technologies. It is no good inventing a wheel if no one realizes that you can turn it. Ditto the e-mail: we have to understand just what it can make possible.

The first section of this book will therefore primarily be about understanding. We will use some hypothetical case studies from 'before' and 'after' the invention of e-mail to gain a vivid grasp of how life has been de-complicated, and the impossible made possible, by the coming of this new communication tool.

Through doing this, we will be able to see how both personal lives and business communications can be transformed by the power of the e-mail.

This section could be classed as providing the conceptual building blocks of writing the perfect e-mail. It is only through appreciating the true significance of the e-mail for communication generally, that we will be in a position to exploit that significance for ourselves and our businesses.

2 Abandoning . . . and Absorbing

Adaptation involves abandoning some of your old beliefs and assumptions. It's all very well being able to appreciate the potential in the new, but if you are still saddled with all your old assumptions about the 'way things are' then you're going to be held back by doubt, fear or just sheer bloody-mindedness. 'I've always done it this way. Why should I change now?'

But, the fact is that nowadays adaptation is no longer a choice, it is a necessity. In a world of constant change, even one's core beliefs must continually be tested and revised.

However, it's all very well abandoning a redundant or outmoded set of viewpoints. The question is, what is to replace them? The process of absorbing new ideas and techniques is in fact inextricably linked to the act of abandoning others. One cannot happen without the other. No one is going to abandon something if they have nothing to replace it with. Would you knock down your house without having a better one to move into?

Therefore the two acts of abandoning and absorbing will be covered together in one central section of the book. We will start by examining a few of the clichés that persist about the e-mail and the Internet in general, and by exposing the sort of assumptions and prejudices that lie behind them. We will challenge the received wisdom about e-mail. By bringing the sober light of clear thinking to bear on the views of e-mail reactionaries, we will make possible the leap forward to an invigorating, fresh approach. The new ideas and techniques will emerge from understanding precisely why the old assumptions have become deficient.

This section will above all focus on our approach to language. From the classroom, many of us have inherited what are virtually an inviolable set of doctrines and strictures about what is acceptable and what isn't. As a result of this, many of us are stuck with some unhelpful ideas and beliefs about syntax, grammar and language more generally.

Adaptation involves absorbing new principles and techniques. So you've put yourself in an open frame of mind, one that is prepared to dispense with old principles. But now you have to take the step of actually being prepared to learn something new, whether it be some fresh ideas about language, or simply the computer software required to use e-mail effectively. This is perhaps the hardest stage of all. It is the truly substantive one; the one that will determine the overall success or failure of your ability to adapt.

Learning to write again
Learning to write the perfect e-mail is not quite like learning a foreign language. Fortunately, the words are the same, and computer software can readily be mastered. So you can quickly put to rest any fears of examinations in the New Laws of E-Grammar and the like.

However, it is a question of learning a new *style* of language, by which we mean one that is stripped of all the contrivances and formulations that were appropriate to the old forms of written communication. With e-mail, functionality becomes far more important. This doesn't mean that elegance or grammatical sense can or should be dispensed with entirely. But we do have to be open to new forms, and to some extent we ourselves have to be responsible for devising them.

In order to take full advantage of the possibilities of the e-mail, we have to learn to think like children. We need their openness, their innocence and, above all, their ability to create.

To us this sounds very exciting. We hope it does to you too.

Let's have a sample of the power of the well-written e-mail and how it scores against it's rival the business letter. Let's say you work for Bigpocket Bank. You've set up an e-bank, but are still working on the functionality. At present the customer can do only a limited a range of things on-line. You get an e-mail asking if you can deal shares on-line. It's not possible yet, but you're working on it. Look how the available informality and speed of the e-mail helps the customer feel better about you.

Many thanks for your e-mail.
You can only carry out share dealing with us by telephone at the moment. We are working on a new service to let you deal with us on-line and it should be ready within the next few months. Thanks for making contact with us. If you need any help the number is 0100 10 20 60. Please do give us a ring. We'll be happy to give you all the help you need.
Kind regards
Steve Morris

This is a winning piece of communication, not necessarily because of what it says, but because of the way it says it. Notice how with the e-mail you can:

- be more personal.
- sound more human.
- deal with people quickly and know the query has been answered.

This is the great promise of the e-mail. It gives people in business, at work, the chance to communicate more in the way they would at home. For too long we have divided so-called professional styles of communication at work and informal styles at home. E-mail feels more like speech and less like writing. It has rhythm and pace. It is engaging.

Switching from Bigpocket Bank. Here are three more modern personal e-mails. Each shows how the medium can add a freshness and zest so often lacking in standard business letters.

Many thanks for your e-mail.
You make some really interesting points about the environment. I can assure you we are fully committed to environmental policies. We recycle as much as we can and we only buy from suppliers with environmental policies that are at least as intouch as ours. Your views are very helpful to us. Thanks again for taking the time and trouble to get in touch.
Kind regards
Steve Morris

Here notice again the human tone but also the:

- Precision. The language is spare without being sparse. Each word earns its place.
- User-friendliness. It feels as though it has been written by a real flesh and blood human.
- The spoken but not too-spoken feel, creating a sense of relationship and engagement.

It has the breath of fresh air about it. It feels more fluid, more genuine.

> Thank you for your e-mail. We're always very keen hear views and comments from customers – it helps us to check our service, and keep improving it. So I'm grateful to you for getting in touch and for what you say.
> Thanks.
> Steve Morris

Here the e-mail allows us to:

- Demonstrate listening. It feels like we care.
- Be warmer then in a traditional letter. Again it feels more spoken and personal.
- Be precise and direct.

And finally

> Hello Mr Morris.
> Many thanks for your very positive comments. It's always good to hear from people, especially when they let us know we are doing things right. Thank you so much for getting in touch and I hope you continue to enjoy visiting us.
> Kind regards

Notice:

- It's much more distilled than a traditional letter. It is sharp and clear.
- It still maintains flavour. It has a distinctive personality.

3 Acting

Last of all, adaptation is about acting. It is all very well having had the vision, then emptying and opening your mind, but in the last resort it all comes down to action. Will you be willing and able to take steps to really make the most out of e-mail? This is equally true for individuals and for companies. In the end, actions speak louder than words, and the test of how successful this book will be is whether it has a real and tangible impact on people's lives. If it does for just a few of you, then we'll be happy indeed.

Appreciating e-mails, abandoning old ideas, absorbing new principles will flow naturally into the task of actually crafting the perfect e-mail time and time again.

However, our understanding of the possibilities of this dynamic form, together with our new receptivity to ideas, will have made us realize that there is in fact no such thing as the perfect e-mail. In fact the possibilities of the e-mail can be exploited in all sorts of ways, many of which have hardly begun to be recognized. E-mails, for example, for the very first time make possible the notion of truly direct marketing; that is, marketing customized perfectly to the individual needs and interests of the recipient, stripped bare of the old hyperbole and 'hard selling'.

But more of that later. All we will promise at this stage is that this book will help you to do something far more valuable than writing the perfect e-mail. It will equip you with the tools – the mind-frame, the concepts, the principles and the language – to be able to write, a perfect e-mail in every single situation in which you need to do so.

We hope you enjoy.

CHAPTER 1

Appreciation: the vision of a new world

In order to appreciate the true significance of the e-mail for communication, we are going to divide this section into 'before' and 'after'. Both sections will use the same hypothetical examples, based on realistic situations, to illustrate the difference between life before and after the coming of the e-mail.

BEFORE

Imagine, for a moment, that the clock has been turned back. The year is 1985, before e-mails have ever even been heard of except by a very few IT experts scattered around a few dusty university faculties and government departments, unobtrusively going about their business. Put yourself in the place of a few people struggling with issues of communication in this strange, bereft world of not so long ago. We have three examples for you, each illustrating a different area (or rather, non-area) of communication in this pre-virtual age.

Example 1: the long-distance family man
You have been sent to South America on an extended

business posting. Your wife and three children are back in England. When the posting came, you thought of bringing them with you, but it wasn't really viable. She has a successful career, which can't easily be transposed abroad. Your children are established in schools you trust, and you want to keep them there. But you miss them all terribly. You want to be able to keep in touch with your family daily. What are you to do?

Three things come to mind.

You spend a fortune on phone bills. It is very nice to hear the voices of your children across crackling, long-distance phone lines. The trouble is that with your work commitments and the time difference, it is always difficult to reach them at a convenient time, and the phone keeps cutting off when you do.

You write letters. Your friends and family tell you how much they enjoy receiving your beautifully crafted, elegant missives, full of lovely phrases and descriptions, but it does take them an awfully long time to arrive. And then when they want to reply they invariably have to check whether you are still in Macchu Picchu or have moved on to Rio de Janeiro. Plus you would so love to be able to keep in touch with your old friend Dave on a daily basis, to find out the latest news on the local team. Not surprisingly, you can't get local English-language papers out here (even the ones from home arrive several days late). You feel very cut off. For the first time, you are beginning to understand the meaning of distance.

You are silent. Perhaps, in the circumstances, the best solution. Certainly the most convenient. Except things get so lonely. If only, you think, I could just press a few buttons, and be in constant touch . . .

Example 2: the dynamic businesswoman
You are a dynamic young project manager, involved in

14

the setting up of a number of hotels and holiday resorts throughout northern Europe. The project is part of the world-wide expansion activities of a well-known American hotel and leisure company: let's call it Lifestyle Plus. Your job is to monitor these developments, making sure they are in line with the company's overall brand values and tone, whilst allowing margin for appropriate local variations.

You are constantly on the move. As well as being in regular communication with all the sites throughout northern Europe, you have to be in almost constant contact with head office in New York. Every day, there are a host of small enquiries – points of detail, fact-checking, opinions on this or that – which need to be verified or confirmed. What's more, in New York there are a host of different departments, staffed by a host of different people and inevitably it seems that every one of your queries has to be dealt with by a different person.

Because of the time-pressures on the project, communicating by mail isn't an option. It is either fax or phone. These are nightmares, though. Most of the time the connections don't seem to be working. Because you are often visiting up to three sites per day, there are endless complications about which number you can be reached on and at which precise moment. Moreover, much of the information that you receive from head office has to be tailored or refined by you, and then distributed among the various European sites. On each occasion this involves a mammoth organizational headache, as you struggle with sheets of paper, telephone and fax contact numbers, not to mention the hassle of doing all this when you are constantly on the move.

It is also so difficult to trace the various people needing to be contacted. They are invariably in meetings, or out to lunch or somewhere unknown. Sometimes they leave contact numbers, sometimes they don't as you can imagine, it is almost worse when they do, simply because it adds to the number of phone and fax numbers on the go.

By the end of the project, you have a severe headache, and swear to yourself never to work on this kind of thing again.

Example 3 (or 'the funny one'): The heat-seeking Eskimo

You are an Eskimo, with an unusual interest in the topography of the sub-Saharan desert region. As you can imagine, it isn't particularly easy, out here in Eskimo-land, to satisfy your curiosity about this wonderfully fascinating subject. For some strange reason, your buddies don't share your interests. When you start telling them about desert scrub life they throw ice at you. Nor do the book shops in your ice district have very large sections on sub-Saharan subjects. In fact, it would be more accurate to say that they don't have any books whatsoever on the subject, and when you gently suggest that they start stocking some they only look at you as if you were a complete lunatic.

Life, as you can imagine, is pretty frustrating. Sometimes you wonder if you really are a lunatic after all, or if you have accidentally been born into the wrong body. Sometimes you dream of running off to some great desert region, and there pursuing your interest to your heart's content. But you know this is fanciful. You have duties here on the ice-farm. Besides, as you know from your one trip south to more temperate climes, you can't actually stand the heat. Your internal thermostat is geared only to accept sub-zero temperatures. Anything above that and you develop heat stroke.

So what are you to do? Fortunately, via a distant

cousin in central Africa, you have established contact with one person who knows about desert topography. He is great, really helpful. Every now and then he sends you parcels containing articles on desert irrigation, little bits of desert scrub, the odd ant or beetle. They never fail to brighten your day. However, you have to wait months between each delivery. And sometimes the contents of the parcels get seized by over-zealous customs officials, who claim that importing dead insects is a violation of Arctic customs regulations. A bit of a bummer, really.

In the end, you accept your fate. It seems clear that you are destined never to satisfy your curiosity about deserts. Deserts are there; you are here. The world is a big place: too big for you and your funny obsession.

Our examples illustrate some fairly crucial deficiencies of communication before the coming of the e-mail. They could easily be multiplied to embrace just about every situation under the sun involving communication.

But this is hardly necessary. It should by now be fairly clear that communication before e-mail was fairly problematic. The thing is, it was *possible*. Letters could be written; telephone calls could be made; faxes could be sent. No job or task was completely prevented by the difficulties of communicating. It's just that everything was difficult and complicated. However you chose to keep in touch, there was always a problem. Phones were expensive, and you had to catch the person in the right place. Faxes were extremely inconvenient to use, and they had to be sent to a specific number and place. Letters solved some of these problems, but were so slow.

It was a world where everything seemed possible on a good day, but more often you were dragged down by a sense of the massive obstacles that had to be overcome.

In particular, getting anything done efficiently over long distance was a near impossibility. Because of this, people were more likely to resign themselves to not even trying. They accepted that communication was basically something that only could go on between people who were close together geographically. Those who did do things on a more international basis had to spend much of their time incommunicado, shuttling around from place to place – and this, as our second example showed, only made the problems of communicating all the more tricky.

So let's remind ourselves of the defining features of the world before e-mail. It was: local, restricted, segmented, complicated isolated.

Of course, some people would say that many of these features are good things. They would say that a world of local, close-knit communities is more secure than one of open access across space and borders. They would say that small communities breed happiness and continuity. By contrast, globalization brings in its wake alienation and loneliness. A world where space is no longer an obstacle to communication is unreal, even fantastical. People will use communication over distance as a substitute for the real thing, which is only possible on a local, face-to-face level. Society will fragment, and our comforts will become increasingly hollow.

This is indeed a pessimistic vision of the future, but it leaves out one important thing: the element of choice. Many people see the expansion of new forms of communication as threatening, because they think that, like a bulldozer, they will completely roll over and wipe out everything that went before. The fear of losing every last aspect of the 'old' is so overriding that it becomes impossible to comprehend that there might possibly be anything good in the 'new'.

This is an unrealistic way of looking at change. When new technologies come along, they do not necessarily replace everything that went before. People will only use them if and when they find them more useful than the old technologies. They are free to decide for themselves. The bottom line is that no one has been, or will be, forced to use e-mail. And even if a person does use it, this does not mean that he or she cannot also use other, older forms of communication.

What the invention of new technologies like e-mail means is greater choice, and choice should never be feared. Just because the e-mail makes instant long-distance communication possible, this does not imply that local communities will fragment, that we will no longer meet anyone except on the Net. It's just that other, new options become possible.

Moreover, people often don't realize that e-mails can even strengthen communication on a local level. (Think of the captain of a football club in a small town, arranging fixtures. No longer the need to meet in the pub at 6 p.m. every Thursday, no need to post up team sheets in a conveniently public place, or for all those phone calls. Just one circular e-mail and it's all done!)

AFTER

The advent of the e-mail and the Internet together is like the squaring of the circle. All the bits that pointed in the right direction before now suddenly seem to have fitted into place. You get that positive sense that now, at last, we have a communication system which makes it possible to do all the things that you wanted to do, but were held back from doing by primitive or complicated technology.

But let's look closely at the attributes that e-mail communication actually has. You'll see that it is a formidable list.

Simple. The simplicity bit speaks for itself. What do you need to be on e-mail? A computer, or access to one. An e-mail address, easily obtained from any web server. And knowledge of some basic software, which can be mastered in less than an hour.

Instant. Whereas a letter has to travel physically to its destination, an e-mail exists as nothing more than a series of electronic signals cruising through telephone wires at an astonishing speed. Sending and arriving are not divided by time.

Non-intrusive. This is important. Phone calls are frankly a bore. They disturb you; they wake you up; they can't be 'put aside' for a moment. Communication by phone means two people being hooked up and attentive to one another at precisely the same moment – one which often isn't convenient for each party. Physical mail is less intrusive, but it still needs to be handled, filed or thrown away. E-mails are accessible at the click of a button, exactly when you want to read them.

Secure. Phone calls can be tapped; letters can be read by anyone whose hands they pass through. Though there have been concerns about Internet security, all the signs are that this is fast improving, and that e-mails will be a comparatively secure form of communication.

Cheap. E-mails are cheap. Simply the cost of a local call to send one, anywhere in the world. Servers won't bust the bank; some (Hotmail for example) are even free. All in all, e-mail represents extraordinarily good value for money.

Environmentally friendly. The environment is not going to suffer. After all, e-mails travel along phone lines that already exist, so no digging and excavation! In addition, they don't require the use of paper, and that can't be bad for rainforests the world over.

Virtual. Finally, e-mails are virtual. What exactly does this mean? This is the most difficult thing to explain, but probably represents the e-mail's single most valuable asset. E-mails, like websites, don't exist in any fixed physical space, but instead reside in that mysterious, intangible sphere known as 'cyberspace'.

Where is this? What is this? Probably the best way of explaining it is to say that it exists both nowhere and everywhere. You can't see cyberspace, or touch it or smell it. In fact, it can't be experienced directly. But we know it exists. How? Because we catch a glimpse of it whenever we switch on a computer and hook up to the Net, whether to visit a website or read our e-mails. Each on-line computer is like a little peephole on to that big, unfathomable world of information.

And the true secret? The real source of its value? It is that *you don't have to be in any one place to access it*. All you need is a computer with a modem and, hey presto, the whole of cyberspace is yours to navigate. It's not simply the volume of information available. It's the fact that it can be reached wherever you are.

To sum up
In the old world of communication, you needed to go to the place where you could be communicated with, at a given time. In the new world, messages are sent to a single address and you can then access them in your own time from wherever you happen to be.

This is communication with the hassle and difficulty taken out of it. It is the communication of the future.

Afterword: where are they now?
Let's return to our fantasy examples and see what

became of them.

You will remember they weren't very happy. But then something came along: E-mails revolutionized every one of their lives – along with the lives of countless others like them.

For the businessman, keeping in touch with his family from South America was no longer a problem. He could chat to his wife and kids on a daily basis. Dave, his old friend, could keep him abreast of all the news from the local team. And he didn't even need to miss his children growing up. With scanning, his wife could send him regular photos with the utmost ease . . . with video conferencing just around the corner!

As for the project manager, these days running multi-national projects isn't such a trial. It's still difficult, of course. There are pressures, tight deadlines, angry clients. But at least now she has one less thing to worry about. Communicating is no longer a difficult business. In fact, it's easy. She's just got one, portable computer, and a list of e-mail addresses. And hey presto, she's in touch with whoever she wants, whenever she needs to be.

But what about the Eskimo? Well, things aren't going quite so fine and dandy. His folks are beginning to get a bit irate. There've been a few harsh words exchanged, even talk of some more drastic measures. It all started to go wrong, you see, when his cousin in Africa, perhaps fed up with sending bits of desert all over the world, one day arranged for a computer to be sent down Eskimo-way. Since then, our Eskimo has seldom been seen. He sits in his darkened room, all hours of the day and night, talking in desert chat rooms, e-mailing mysterious fellow Sahara enthusiasts.

Actually, his friends and family are worried as well as angry. He shirks his duties, doesn't seem to appreciate their way of life at all. They always thought he was a bit odd, but now he really seems to have lost it. E-mails, you see, don't always work for everyone. Perhaps because they are so darn useful, other people can get a bit jealous. But at least our Eskimo is happy.

And maybe that's the most important thing of all!

CHAPTER 2

Abandoning old ideas, absorbing new ones

Let's start off with a few things that are sometimes said about e-mail.

- E-mails are easy to write. They require no thought.
- The e-mail is really just a letter on a computer. It doesn't need to be approached differently in any way.
- E-mails won't have any impact whatsoever on business. The old forms of communication will still predominate.
- E-mails are all the same. See one, you've seen them all.
- E-mails aren't for everyone. They belong to a world very different from the normal one. What have I got in common with a cyber-geek? I don't want to live in the global village. I'm very happy with where I live right now.

If you look at these viewpoints closely, you'll see that they all have one, striking thing in common: a blanket refusal to accept the world in any form other than that in which it has existed in the past. The refusal to accept change is one of the most absurd points of view that it is possible to have. It constitutes nothing less than a total denial of our existence. For if nothing had ever changed, we would never have developed from apes, apes would never have developed from more primitive life forms, and so on, back to the time when there was nothing. Change is the most basic fact of our existence. We should never deny it.

Let's now take each of the statements above, and give it a subtext, or implied meaning. You will see how each one has an underlying assumption, each representing a different weapon in the reactionary game-plan.

- 'E-mails are easy to write': *trivialize the change.* By trivializing something, we reduce it, and therefore make it less significant. The underlying message: e-mails are for stupid, shallow people who can't be bothered to make the effort to communicate properly.
- 'The e-mail is really just a letter': *deny the change.* Out-and-out denial is always one possible course. The underlying message is: letters are what have been, what are and what always will be. They can never be replaced. Therefore when something threatens to replace it, we must simply call it a letter as well.
- 'E-mails won't have a serious impact': *underestimate the change.* Even if you don't deny it, you can always underestimate it. By doing this you can make change seem less wide-reaching, or important than it really is. The underlying message is: e-mails will be important only in unimportant areas – private intercourse and the like. In what really matters, i.e. business, traditional modes of communication will remain indispensable.
- 'E-mails are all the same': *belittle the change.* Keep it

25

under control by limiting its potential. The message is: e-mails are limited, inflexible, unvaried, one-dimensional. All in all, a very insubstantial medium.

- 'E-mails are for cyber-geeks': *compartmentalize the change.* Change seems more manageable if we hive it off, and draw distinctions between who it is and isn't for. The underlying message is: e-mails are somehow unrespectable, suitable only for social outcasts and reprobates.

Not for the likes of me! – in other words.

Reality-check: the truth about e-mails
In the last section, we looked at some of the ways in which the e-mail can be and has been resisted by companies and individuals. We saw that rejecting or belittling it went with a certain mindset, based on an insistence that any possible benefits would be more than negated by their corrupting influence on the existing channels of communication. From the 'decline of language' through to doubting that the e-mail would prove a useful tool of business communication, we saw what a depressing view of the new technology a few negative statements could produce.

The question is, what steps can be taken to overcome these rigid attitudes? As the saying goes, you can't teach an old dog new tricks, and when it comes to the Internet many individuals and companies leap to the conclusion that they are indeed 'old dogs' who can't be turned into technological innocents.

We do agree that there is a certain amount of intractability which simply cannot be undone. If people are disposed to close their minds off completely to something new, then in the last resort one only has to leave them to their beliefs. Ultimately, the good of the many can't be sacrificed to the requirements of the few. If reactionaries don't actively prevent others from moving on, then finally one has to draw the line and leave them to their old assumptions, safe in the knowledge that they won't be doing everyone else any great harm.

But we firmly believe that this approach of 'live and let live' is only really necessary in a small minority of cases. We think that many of those who do adopt a reactionary attitude to change are not quite as intractable as they seem. For the impulse to resist change is often based less on substantive opinion or argument, than on a simple, basic *fear of letting go.* People are frightened of change not because of what the change actually means, but simply because it means change. For some people, just the word itself is enough to produce a reaction somewhere between fear and hostility, even before they have given any serious thought to what the change will actually entail.

The result is a total inability to think things through clearly.

CHAPTER 3

Acting – or putting your learning into practice

In this chapter we are going to look at some of the organisational issues around e-mail.

I recently worked for a large rail company. Six years ago they employed one person two mornings a week to handle their customer complaints and comments mail. Gradually the mountain began to grow. These days the company receives 1,500 letters a week and a similar number of e-mails. It employs six people in its customer care department and the piles of letters rarely seem to get any smaller.

The message is that e-mails won't go away. And e-mails in particular do pose some serious organizational issues.

1   SPEED

People will wait a few weeks for the answer to a letter. They expect an answer to an e-mail within hours. The whole e-mail environment is based on speed. They e-mail back their friends and colleagues within minutes. They will find it hard to understand why a company cannot do the same. But to do so causes a systems, management and staff resources problem. It also creates some interesting challenges for the bottom line. Answering an e-mail is quick and less cumbersome than a traditional letter (so costs are lower here) but to answer it speedily requires very flexible staff resources and systems (which can be more costly).

So what are the answers to the problem of customer expectations? Put simply they are these:

Companies need to use the most effective IT system and server possible. You need to get the e-mail quickly and give yourself as high chance as possible to send it quickly.

Standardization is the only route. It is expensive and slow having individual operators answering each e-mail individually. It is more than possible to develop a library system to standardize as many replies as possible. Our research has shown that there is a key piece of customer behaviour in favour of this approach: where letters from customers often contain convoluted problems and lots of padding the classic customer e-mail is simpler, direct and to the point. Rather than writing to tell you that they've had a nice day and ate an egg sandwich and their father's father was a customer of yours all those years ago and by the way you forgot to read the meter last Friday, the e-mail is likely to be a one liner: 'Why didn't you read my meter last Friday?'

This means it's easier to sort the e-mails and to send relatively standard, brief but personal e-mails in return.

A step-by-step guide to developing an e-mail library
Your likely first response to this will be 'we can't – our customers write to us about so many things that we have to answer them individually'. That's where we all start from, but it's a misconception.

- Begin with where you are right now. Take one week of e-mails you receive, and analyse them thoroughly. Work out the volume and then begin to categorize them under content headings. Start broad and then narrow down. The end result should be piles of e-mails all organized into content areas. Be as specific as possible. For example:

Complaints
Requests for information
Useful customer suggestions
Policy issues
Personnel issues

Your second analysis might break down the categories further. For instance:

Complaints
    about service
    about quality
    about price
    about availability

Requests for information
    about your company generally
    about a specific operational area
    about a product or service you offer

Useful customer suggestions
    new business idea
    suggestions for operational changes
    suggestions for product or service improvements

Policy issues
    what's your company's policy on the environment?
    what's your company's policy on smoking?

Personnel issues
    do you have any vacancies?
    can I sell you consultancy services?

These are general categories. Only you know your

company well enough to see which general categories fit and where you can introduce company-specific categories.

- Look at what out-going e-mails you have already developed. Try to find an existing e-mail for as many of the content areas as possible. If there is more than one per area, no problem. Collect everything; quality control comes later.
- Do the quality check. For each area pick the best e-mail you have. Any e-mails that seem to generate repeat complaints from customers – about the tone or content – deposit in the bin. At the end of this process you'll know where you have effective e-mails and where you have gaps.
- Fill the gaps. Where you have gaps write fresh e-mails.
- Edit everything. It's important to have a consistent style throughout. So, take all the e-mails you've narrowed down to and edit them. Aim for a consistent tone and style in the following:

  Signing on and signing off. Adopt some conventions about saying hello and goodbye (we have some suggestions about this later in the book).

  Name. How are you going to write the recipient's name and your own? In full, first name only?

  Terms. If you are using certain terms regularly agree on how to use them.

  Style. Don't switch from the friendly to the formal.

The next step is to agree a way of naming and coding the different sections. Your naming convention should be easy to use and easy to remember. Don't let your IT people take over on this. We've had experience of perfectly sensible alphanumeric codes (like COMP1 for the first in the series of complaints letters) being changed to 7 digit numeric codes like 0007321 where 00 signifies complaints, 073 the particular product area in question, 21 the type of complaint (such as staff rudeness). From an IT perspective, all this makes eminent sense and keeps the system open so you can add more codes in the future. From a user's point of view, it's unwieldy, unmemorable and a complete nightmare. So we recommend a coding system that's alphanumeric, short, easy to use and suggestive of the content.

Finally, the question: database, intranet or simple library?

How you code your e-mails depends on what system you're going to use. There are three options, each with advantages and disadvantages.

Option	Advantages	Disadvantages	Types of Cost
Database (like Microsoft Access)	It's a readily available, standard PC programme that will be compatible with your existing suite of programmes.	Databases can be costly to set up because they usually require a dedicated database person.	Program cost
		Database programmes are not known for being user-friendly to set up or maintain. It can also be difficult to manoeuvre between one file and another.	Programming costs

Option	Advantages	Disadvantages	Types of Cost
Intranet (an internal internet for your company)	It's an intuitive system, that allows you to search keywords and areas. The search function, like the search function on the wider internet, is a very powerful tool.	This is a costly and time-consuming option, requiring a whole host of professionals: IT professionals, Designers, Programmers. It needs continual programming support to maintain and update. Depending on your existing IT system, you may have to buy new hardware to run it.	Programmer costs Design costs On-going maintenance costs Hardware costs
Simple library on PC	It's immediate, works in the program your writers are familiar with, can be changed without needing specialist help, can grow organically.	Keeping a large file on programmes such as Word can be a problem, as large files may collapse or corrupt. Regular backups are needed. The search function is rudimentary, and not as effective as either of the other options.	Secretarial time to save the library in a single file.

By far the simplest, quickest option is to build a simple library on your PC. This is how it works if you're using Microsoft Word (other programmes are similar)

- Build and save your library as one Word file.
- Each standard letter must have its own code.
- Use edit, find to bring up the search text box. Type in what you want to find, such as your first complaints letter COMP1.
- Click on find next to take you directly to this standard letter in the file.
- Close the find box.

2   CONTROL

Sometimes e-mail runs wild. People use it for so many different purposes: to crack jokes, gossip, sort out social arrangements, tell everyone the new baby is called Bill. Unfortunately they sometimes do all this at work, which is where the trouble starts.

Unsurprisingly, then, companies break out in a cold sweat because the network is so uncontrolled and damaging. Where people would huddle around the coffee machine to gossip, they now frequently do it by e-mail. The big difference is that spoken words are often forgotten, but the e-mail is written down, making it a far more significant force.

It is also very hard to control, and with the proliferation of intranets and extranets this control becomes even more problematic. Some might say there's no point trying to control the uncontrollable, but we believe there are some sensible steps to take.

Controlling the use of email
Companies often have protocols for staff behaviour in key areas. For instance, staff are often trained in answering the phone, dealing with the public, and how to use the company's property. Rarely are they trained in using e-

mails correctly. This is important because there's a perception problem with e-mail. Because people often have free access to the Internet at home, they assume e-mail is either free or at a negligible cost to their company. Sending personal messages is not seen as pilferage in the same way as franking personal postal mail might be.

This isn't a trivial matter. Think, for example, of messages being sent to or received from inappropriate destinations: would you want your company to be in 'contact' with extreme political groups? Resources are wasted in the shape of staff time and unprofitable additions to the phone bill.

Efficiency is compromised at the system becomes blogged with trivial personal chitter-chatter . . . not to mention the risk of receiving messages that may contain viruses.

The solution is to produce some guidelines for the use of e-mail and train people how to use it – and when not to.

Controlling content
It's bad enough that one of your employees might send an e-mail to someone your organization isn't in sympathy with. That the content may be libellous, racist, discriminatory or promoting acts that are downright illegal is truly beyond the pale. Imagine the damage, for instance that an e-mail from a Body Shop employee to the Countryside Alliance about how much they were looking forward to being in at the kill at the next fox hunt might cause if it became public. And if you think this is unlikely, you'd be wrong. It didn't happen to the Body Shop but it did happen to a company we know of. The press is ready and waiting to exploit inconsistencies in any company's public and private face. The simple e-mail has increasingly provided the raw material for negative press stories.

Much more likely, though, is the e-mail response to a customer that is rude, that may invite legal action because it admits liability, that is racist or discriminatory, or just plain wrong. How can you control quality issues like these? You may be responding only to a relatively small number of e-mails each day, and you may be able to check them. A company we have worked with does employ a team of supervisors to vet each and every e-mail before it goes out, but that's quite an undertaking and clearly is a cost they are prepare to bear; if you're sending hundreds of e-mails a day, then of course checking each one becomes less possible.

There is, though, an answer: set some rules.

- Who can e-mail and to whom. This is helpful because it stops misunderstandings.
- What is and isn't acceptable content. Makes things crystal clear and gives you a standard by which to judge behaviour.
- Who checks what. Allows for firm lines of command.
- What are the sanctions if the rules are broken. Warning, dismissal?
- Where e-mails will be stored.
- What to do if you suspect e-mails are being misused.

Using e-mails inside an organization

We wouldn't be surprised if the companies that make internal memo pads have gone out of business, such is the change in getting messages around companies. These days, most companies use internal e-mail and the secretaries who used to type out, photocopy and deliver internal memos are breathing huge sighs of relief, and using the extra time wisely at the coffee station.

It may be an easier, faster way of communicating,

but it's not without its drawbacks. Here are a few and how to avoid them.

Death by e-mail

After a period of two days' leave, I came back to find 103 e-mail messages waiting for me. Many of them were flagged as needing an urgent response, so I started opening them first. Of the forty or so urgent ones, only one or two really needed my immediate attention. Even then, I found out about the most important task I should do that morning from a handwritten message on a post-it note stuck to my phone by my chief executive! It took me the best part of a morning to open, read, print off and file my e-mails. Many were totally unnecessary and I found myself resenting my machine and hunting for the plug to disconnect it.

This is a common problem. It's so easy to send an e-mail and copy it to all and sundry that it's often done without any thought. This is a real problem for people who are already busy. So when should you send an e-mail and who should you send it to?

The rules of engagement

Before you log on, ask yourself a few simple questions:

What do I need to communicate? It may be the date of a meeting, your draft customer care policy, appraisal notes for your last appraisal, whatever.

Who do you need to communicate with? Obviously, with the person you're sending it to. But does it need to go to that person's line manager, secretary, co-worker or chief executive too? You should only copy your e-mails to other people on **a strictly need-to-know basis**. Ask yourself whether it would impair the other person's ability to do their job if they didn't receive a copy of your e-mail. If the answer is no, then don't copy them in.

Take this as an example.

To	John
From	Sue
Subject:	new meeting date

John
I've cancelled the meeting on the 5th you couldn't make for your appraisal and re-scheduled it for 16th June at 10am in my office.
Sue

On the face of it, a simple one-to-one communication. But, if Sue doesn't copy it to the team secretary, he or she won't know not to book other meetings for them on that day. It may also be appropriate for Sue to copy in the personnel manager, so that he or she may decide whether to attend or not. It would be completely unnecessary for Sue to copy in the other seventeen members of the team.

Should you use e-mail at all?

If in the old days before e-mail you would have picked up the phone and spoken to someone, then phone them rather than e-mail them. Nothing is more irritating than receiving an e-mail about something you'd expect to be asked face to face. One of my employees, sitting less than four feet away, e-mailed me to ask if he could take the afternoon off to go to the dentist. I didn't receive the e-mail until about an hour before he wanted to leave and replied simply, 'Come and ask me'. After a brief chat about the correct use of e-mail he went off for his appointment.

Have you got the timing of your e-mail right?

E-mail is an almost instantaneous form of communication. No sooner have you clicked *Send* than it's there on the recipient's machine. Human beings are not quite so predictable. Just because you've sent it doesn't mean they've read it, so make sure you send your message in good time.

E-mail as a means of defence
Imagine how you'd feel receiving this e-mail.

To	Christine
From	Peter
cc	Graham W, Susan, Ross, Michelle, Joe S, Robert, Manuel, Adrian, Joshua, Neena, Sheila M, Nathan, Linda, Cyrus, Mark G, Mark W, Jatinder
Subject	last night's tenants' meeting

I had a complaint from the chair of the tenants' association about the way yesterday's meeting went. You obviously need to be much more organized in the way you approach these things to stop them becoming a shambles. In future, I want to see your agenda before the meeting and your plan for making it happen. We need to dissect what happened – my office tomorrow at 9 o'clock sharp please.

Possibly the original complaint was justified but your manager's response isn't. It is abrupt and judgemental but also exposes your supposed failings to Graham W, (your Chief Executive), Susan, (your departmental head) and all of your colleagues. To put it mildly, you wouldn't be very happy.

How to respond, though? Should you launch into a spirited defence and send it to all the same people or rise above it and send a pertinent, factual reply to Peter?

Sending a response to everyone just perpetuates the problem of irrelevant material being sent inappropriately. Better to avoid arguing in public and to follow the rule above of only e-mailing people who actually need to know.

There are times when sending an e-mail message as proof that you are being proactive and doing your job is an important weapon in your defence. It's a good way of recording and assigning responsibilities in a task involving several people. Copying e-mails of this nature to senior managers is a useful way of upping the tempo: by raising expectations that certain actions will take place, the people they are assigned to often feel compelled to get on with it. Like the adage says, the only jobs to get done are those you like doing, are good, at or the ones your boss wants you to do straightaway.

E-mail as offence

E-mail is a very good tool of self-promotion, if used effectively and sparingly.

Your manager and chief executive may be impressed by some of your work and initiatives but they certainly won't want to be copied in every time you have a thought.

You may want to use the influence of senior staff to get rid of blockages within the organization and that's when copying them is particularly useful. The blockage may be, for instance, your immediate manager. Sending him or her an e-mail asking for assistance copied to their manager is a more subtle and effective way of dealing with the problem than moaning about it with your colleagues.

Fighting the virus-mongers

E-mails have become the front-line in the war between cyber-terrorists and capitalism. At least that's one way of looking at it. Others simply see the virus-mongers as anti-social saddos with nothing better to do. Whatever the case, you have to take the e-mail worm viruses very seriously. The LOVEBUG of 2000 cost businesses millions as it rampaged through the world's computers. Just clicking on the I LOVE YOU icon led to millions of corrupted files and e-mail systems crashing. So what can you do about it?

There is no easy answer, but extreme caution about opening e-mails must be the watchword. With the benefit of hindsight the LOVEBUG was easy to spot. Who normally receives love messages by e-mail?! But the senders of these viral worms have become more and more devious. Here are just three of the viral e-mails and the way they masquerade as real e-mails.

Mothers Day Order Confirmation.
I thought you might like to see this.
Extremely URGENT: To All E-Mail Users.

And so on. The last one here was the way the dreaded Melissa worm attacked. The middle one the Irok.Trojan.Worm. And there will be more.

Every organization needs to put a system in place to guard against such viruses. This could include:

- Checking an anti-virus site at the start and end of each working day for any alerts.
- Keeping anti-virus software up-to-date.
- Never opening anything that looks suspicious.
- Deleting all previous e-mails at the end of each day.
- Renewing e-mail address books regularly.
- Looking out for obviously non-grammatical subject lines. This seems to have been a feature of recent viral worms.

41

- If you receive a suspicious e-mail delete it immediately without opening it.
- Share anti-viral news and warning with colleagues and colleague-organizations.

None of these are guaranteed to work, but they will make the risk of virus infection lower.

3   BRAND

The final element of these organizational issues is brand. At present the e-mail is often the Cinderella of the communications world, dashed off and sometimes unloved. But, in fact, any e-mail needs to reflect and reinforce your brand in its content, style, and speed of delivery.

Now, many businesses, especially smaller ones, say they don't have a brand. But this isn't true. Every business has a brand even if it doesn't know it. A brand is simply a promise. You see the logo, you hear the voice at the end of the phone, you receive the e-mail, you buy the product and it plays a part in the way you feel about the business.

If you look at it with a negative example the point is made. Let's say you are a fun company – Wild-drinking Holidays.Com. You pride yourself that you offer the maddest holidays on the web. You pride yourself that dealing with you is personal and lively and amusing, that the service feels unique. You pride yourself on all these things and then you send the following e-mail to a customer who has just booked a fun-filled weekend in Amsterdam.

Dear customer
With reference to your booking for the 29-30th May inclusive, it is confirmed that you will fly Dunderhead Airways. Please be appraised that your legal terms and conditions will be sent under separate cover.
Assuring you of our good intentions at all times.
James G Morgan Mr

It happens: the brand values and identity here are undercut by the simple e-mail. This e-mail doesn't say fun. It says dusty, civil service. It says 'we should have booked with someone else'. It has many of the features of the traditional business letter. It almost looks as if the person who wrote it had Victorian English as their mother tongue. It would undercut any zappy and expensive advertising. Strange that such a simple thing as an e-mail could say so much about the organization.

So just how do you write an e-mail that is on-brand? Well, there is a process which we look at a little later. But first let's see how Wild-drinking Holidays.Com could have been more on-brand. How about:

Hi Steve
Just to confirm we've booked you in for the weekend of the 29-30 May and you'll be flying Dunderhead Airways. We'll send you the legal terms separately.
Have fun.
James Morgan

This encapsulates the brand. It says we're not stuffy.

We put you first. We want you to have fun. And it reads like a sharp modern e-mail too.

What follows is a step-by-step guide to creating on-brand e-mails.

Keeping e-mails on-brand

Firstly, of course, KNOW YOUR BRAND. Self-evidently, you can't write on-brand without knowing what the brand is. It may be that your company has written notes of brand values and personality. If so, get them and learn them by heart. You may need to approach the marketing department or the brand department. A company mission statement is also a good place to get the big picture about what your company stands for. If you don't have brand values then you'll need to develop a feel for your company stands for.

For instance, your company may stand for good times, reliability, fun, dependable advice. You choose. But the aim is to get a feel for what the promise is. At the end of this process you should be able to complete the following phrase. **When a customer buys our goods or services they know they will get . . .**

When you have a feel for the brand values, try to ADD SOME WORDS THAT BRING THIS BRAND PROPOSITION TO LIFE. So, let's say you work for the holiday company, words that might help you to express the brand more fully could include: fun, lively, unstuffy, modern. personal, adventurous and so on. Then brainstorm a list of things you aren't. Things you aren't would probably include stuffy, pompous, stiff, dull. Make a list of the two sets of words. Now you have something to judge your e-mails on. List one gives you what you are aiming at. List two is do not pass go. For each e-mail you can run through the list and decide whether it encapsulates the good words and ignores the bad words.

Now you have the list, WRITE SOME SAMPLE E-MAILS IN THE NEW TONE OF VOICE. This is likely to take some time. It is wise to do this with others, because you can share creative ideas. It is very likely that you will need to write and edit your samples a number of times to get it just right. And when you've done this it makes sense to test out the results with trusted colleagues and customers. Ask – does this sound like us?

The aim here is to come up with, say, five, really on-brand e-mails that capture in tone what you are and what you stand for. It might be helpful to collect up five e-mails that aren't what you're aiming for so you have a comparison. The aim is to be able to be really certain exactly why an e-mail is on brand – what language features it has and why it encapsulates the brand. Let's take the e-mail from earlier as an example:

Hi Steve

Just to confirm we've booked you in for the weekend of the 29-30 May and you'll be flying Dunderhead Airways. We'll send you the legal terms separately.

Have fun.

James Morgan

Why is this on-brand? For a start, it feels really light and accessible. Just what you'd expect from Wild-drinking Holidays.Com. It uses modern language. There are contractions, personal pronouns and the active voice. It has a touch of zest about it with the 'have fun' line. It is unstuffy. When you've developed this kind of style and an understanding of why particular e-mails are on-brand, you can move on.

START STORING your benchmark e-mails, and adding

to them, in a library. Always check back against your lists and brand values to make sure you haven't drifted too far from your ideas of what constitutes on-brand.

Then WRITE A BRIEF GUIDE TO WRITING E-MAILS ON-BRAND. Include the lists and the brand words and show your examples. The aim is to get a user's guide to your style. This guide can be circulated to everyone writing e-mails. It will act as a central resource as you go about the job of generating a consistent approach. The guide's job is to put into words how to write e-mails. It could include sections like: why we made this change, what is our brand, why our new e-mails sum us up, examples of before-and-after e-mails. Highlight parts of the text that most sum up the new style along with an explanation of why they do.

It may be helpful here to have a do-and-don't list.

Do
- Use good strong active verbs: I will, we will, we have, you can, you should.
- Think of your e-mail as really fresh.
- Make your e-mail sound more conversational.
- Write in full sentences: 'Here's the information you asked for' is more respectful (and grammatically sound) than 'Information follows'.
- Use contractions like I'm, we'll and we're.
- Keep it really short.
- Aim for a sentence length of not more than 15 words.
- Sign all e-mails with your first and last name.

Don't
- Rush your response by: sending an e-mail full of spelling mistakes and inaccuracies (this gives a very sloppy impression to the receiver) or responding

spontaneously and rashly, especially in anger (e-mails can be very hot property and can be copied).

- Write as you would in a normal business letter, so avoid: beginning your e-mail with 'Dear Sir' or 'Dear Mrs X', continuing 'I'm writing to let you know', or signing off with 'Yours faithfully' or 'Yours sincerely'. All these give a feeling of dustiness.
- Use computing abbreviations, such as IOW for 'in other words' and OTOH for 'on the other hand'.
- Get slangy.
- Use unnecessary capitals.

Then RUN SOME TRAINING to make sure everyone involved understands the new rules. Convene a workshop and make sure people understand why you've changed the e-mails, what you are aiming for and how the new style works. Then get participants to practise writing in the new style. Give clear feedback and practise again. When people understand the new brand style you can let them loose on the world.

A typical training day could include: an introduction to the brand, a session on why you've changed the style and then lots of writing exercises on things like ironing out jargon, making your writing more personal and so on.

The style should be fully participative. It often works to break the task of writing down into chunks. So start by writing introductions, move on to main content and then brainstorm ways of concluding.

CHAPTER 4

E-nough already!
Forms of wrongness

Let's start this rule-obsessed chapter with an apologue, or moral fable. It's a gentle, poignant tale about being human wrestling with rules . . . and defining wrongness.

In 1980s university faculties, post-structuralism was the Big Thing. (We're talking British universities now – like other seditious continental ideas, post-structuralism had to serve the standard ten-year quarantine before being allowed across the Channel.) Post-structuralism's dead precursor, structuralism had got all washed up as a scientific theory, mainly because there was no primary object to analyse.

The problem was this: value-free scientific models, previously trusted to shed light on social practices (linguistic, cultural, anthropological), came to be seen as *always-already-interpreted*. So your 'scientific' analysis turned out to be worm-ridden by assumptions. Factors you'd excluded to define your object more precisely, turned out to constitute the object itself.

Instead of looking at a pristine world through an Enlightenment microscope, you were looking at your own face through a maze of cracked mirrors. So structuralism failed, just like Paris '68, and its bitterly self-critical offspring followed in its wake. Where structuralism had been rationally assertive, post-structuralism was unstable and tentative. Where structuralism had confidently known its object, post-structuralism was full of self-undermining and dark desires. Where structuralism looked out at the world, post-structuralism looked into, and up, its own demoralized discourse.

One of its stalwarts, the philosopher Jacques Derrida, had not just a stonking great intellect but also an impish sense of humour. He was interviewed one sunny day about this world of shifting sands where things were never quite what they were. If there was no absolute truth, asked the interviewer, what can we trust? Well, said Derrida, there used to be a truth, except it's all we have and it doesn't work.

He was then asked: if there are no stable meanings, can there be such a thing as an interpretation that is wrong?

At this he paused. (The answer for any self-respecting academic must be yes, but here was a person who proceeded by crossing-out words, leaving both the words and the crossings-out on the page). Gazing into the interviewer's face with an open expression, he answered:

'Erm . . . there are *forms of wrongness*'.

The moral of the story? Well, like post-structuralism, e-mail is regarded by some as a subversive threat, an alien technology threatening our stable world. These folk crave the safe world of known objects, where a spade is a spade, the good is good, and the bad are other people.

To them, e-mail is the new – the Other.

Ignore the fact that it shares plenty in common with other written communications. To the threatened, it's unknown, unpredictable and indeterminate. There are no hard rules. So what do we do in a world where there is no God, no stable authority, no tablets of the law, no rules? We make them up as we go along . . .

All well and good. But there are nonetheless *forms of wrongness*.

E-WRONGNESS: A CONCRETE EXAMPLE

Some people argue, 'If there are no rules, anything is acceptable'. Fortunately, this is not so. For a business to bark at its customers, breathe intrusively down their necks, buttonhole them, or TALK TO THEM AS THOUGH THEY WERE STUPID, can never be acceptable.

If traditional direct mail does all these things, wouldn't you expect its modern e-equivalent to be more clued-up, more carefully honed, more suited to the needs of its customer? You would? Well, we're about to introduce you to some forms of wrongness.

Here's an e-mail that turned up recently on our virtual business site – the equivalent of that pile of litter that lands on your doormat each day. We've doctored this beautiful document just enough to avoid the libel lawyers, so we can take a closer look at how *not* to write on the Internet.

As you read it, think about this new medium which offers businesses the chance to use a more personalized, warm, respectful tone of voice.

Do you feel this virtual mailing succeeds?

From: Axxis Internet Sent: Thu 16/02/2000 16:04
To: Axxis Internet User:;
Subject: Amazing FREE offer from Axxis Internet for February

Axxis Internet are going WAP crazy in February!
By now, you've probably heard about WAP.
You've probably heard about the new PsychoBoy
Internet Phone. And we're willing to bet you'll
probably want to hear about your chance to win
one!

For the month of February, on whichever day you
use the Axxis Internet ISP service for dial-up
Internet access, you will automatically be entered
into a free daily draw for one of the amazing
PsychoBoy Internet Phones. It really is that simple.
What if you're mad keen to win a WAP phone but
you aren't using Axxis Internet for your dial-up
internet access? Well then, all you have to do is
create and use an Axxis Internet 'dial-up net-
working' account – a process we've made really
easy by describing EXACTLY what you have to
do!

Click here for a step-by-step guide . . .

If you'd rather have someone talk you through the
process of setting up an Axxis Internet dial-up
account, you'll be glad to know that for the whole
of February you can call a special 0800 freephone
number where we're ready and waiting to help you
do just that. We can even help you if you have an
account already but you've forgotten your user-
name or password.

Call 0800 784635 for your free help! Or, call the
Axxis Internet Customer Care team by dialling
7532 from your PsychoBoy mobile phone.

Calls to 7532 are charged at MF PsychoBoy RRP
(inc VAT), 45p per minute.

For full details of the PsychoBoy Internet Phone
February Prize Draw Terms & Conditions see

http://promos.axxis. co.uk/wap
Get set-up. Get hooked-up. Get Wapped with Axxis!

UNSUBSCRIBE
You have received this e-mail because you have registered for Axxis Internet. If you do not wish to receive e-mails from Axxis Internet in the future, simply send a blank e-mail to axxis.unsubscribe@ axxismail.co.uk and we will promptly remove your name from future mailings.

Ten questions for 'prospects' like us
Here are ten questions that we, as lovers of the professional e-mail and consumer 'prospects' for virtual marketers, need to know the answers to.

1 Is this message personal?
2 Is it suited to the medium?
3 Does it know its customer?
4 Does it show them a proper, professional respect?
5 Does it make assumptions?
6 Does it give clear information?
7 Is the tone measured?
8 Is the tone consistent?
9 What sort of corporate personality does it reflect?
10 Would you buy a used car from this person?

Answers

Questions 1-4	Nope, not at all
Question 5	Big time
Questions 6-8	No
Question 9	One with scabby warts on
Question 10	Well, *would* you?

Analysing the tone of voice

Before we get to the e-mail proper, something ominous has already been given away in the address section.

It's what the Joe Mantegna character in David Mamet's *House of Games* would call a 'tell' – a minor slip that's actually laden with profound significance. In this e-mail, the small flaw at the start is later writ large in the body copy. It says:

To: Axxis Internet User:;

Ignoring the weirdly inaccurate punctuation of colon *and* semi-colon, this immediately betrays the fact that our virtual mailing has been targeted at . . . no one in particular. Without the slightest forethought, it's simply been hacked together and punted out to that, anonymous mass of unknown prospects – that's customers like you and me.

There's **no attempt to personalize** the letter. No one has taken the trouble to reveal to this company that customers appreciate personal gestures, even while they know the communication cannot be truly one-to-one.

Unfortunately, the entire letter goes on to amplify and reinforce this initial tell – an opening as disastrous in its way as the classic 'To our valued customer'. Customers judge by actions and they know that **clichés** like this really mean the opposite of what they claim.

Next we have the **over-revved** announcement:

Amazing FREE offer from Axxis Internet for February

and immediately we know we're in the realm of traditional direct mail, with the shouted CAPITALS and the hyperbolic *amazing*: **hackneyed devices** which suggest that the offer is actually too poor to be described plainly.

Most people agree that hype conceals information. It sheds more heat than light, distracts readers and acts as a kind of smokescreen for sellers. Did no one tell these e-mail writers that the web is different from traditional delivery channels and that customers can click off in a second? Why on earth have they assumed that this shallow style of writing can be transferred warts and all from the physical world?

Axxis Internet are going WAP crazy in February!

Oh dear. They're pouring on the tired old failsafes – the **overheated tone** (excitable *about a product?*), matey **slang** and colloquialisms, and **exclamation marks** at the end of every other line. And how do we like the idea of this company 'going crazy' over a product? Does it impress us with their judgement, expertise and professionalism? Or does it make us think that, as an organisation, they're probably **self-focused** and a bit **juvenile**? Their letter continues in the same vein:

By now, you've probably heard about WAP. You've probably heard about the new PsychoBoy Internet Phone. And we're willing to bet you'll probably want to hear about your chance to win one!

Not satisfied with making the odd **unwarranted assumption**, they decide to ram the point home with a treble whammy, each building on a **contrived scenario** that gets more and more remote from the customer as it unfolds ('You've probably heard . . . you'll probably want to hear . . .!') This tone continues later, when apparently

. . . you'll be glad to know that for the whole of February you can call a special 0800 freephone number . . .

The tone is **offensively matey** – '. . . And we're willing to bet . . . !' 'Well then, all you have to do . . .' – especially since, just five lines earlier, they couldn't even be bothered to work out our name. But now that the sell is on, we're their best friend.

We're also, unfortunately, really stupid – not just because of the BIG KEY MESSAGES, the exclamation marks, and the hype, but also because of the **patronizing** phrasing. Everything is spelt out in stilted Janet and John sentences, reminding us how *simple* everything is, simply because we're a simple person:

For the month of March . . . it really is that simple . . . Well then, all you have to do . . . a process we've made really easy . . . describing EXACTLY what you have to do!

Just how stoopid are these customers exactly?

The effect of wrongness in e-mails

With a tone that's as wildly inconsistent as this – and you can see how unstable it is by running your eyes over the words highlighted in our last few paragraphs – a company shows that it misunderstands itself as well as its customers. It doesn't know its own values, let alone how these should be expressed in e-writing.

For a start, this communication shouldn't have been put on the web in the first place: it looks and reads as though it was torn from a conventional below-the-line DM campaign. It's a conventional-length letter, and no one reads conventional-length letters on the web; you can spot them a mile off and they never work. So producing e-mails is not as easy as chucking all your existing communications on to the screen with an occasional adjustment. Companies have to customize them, so that they suit their medium as well as their customers.

All these messages are written into the letter, not foisted on it. The sad thing is that they become a concrete part of the company's brand personality. So, instead of sounding and feeling like a customer-focused, warm, friendly, accessible organization, communications like this conjure up an image of some mad-eyed street-seller trying to hawk his stuff to anyone who'll be buttonholed.

When it comes to forms of wrongness in your electronic tone of voice, this outfit should have the market cornered. In fact, it's one of many companies who think their customers appreciate a sudden assault on the senses.

A final wrongness. It is important to use the e-mail channel wisely. Although e-mail marketing is in its infancy, the perpetrators of the 'art' need to tread carefully. People like their e-mails, especially at home. They associate it with friends getting in touch, good times and fun. So when companies take liberties it is all the more annoying; bombarding individuals with unasked-for e-mails and newsletters is to say the least questionable.

The Devil's guide to e-mails
So can we distil what makes a horrible e-mail? Some features are obvious:

- The stilted and stiff. Given the fresh new start we get with e-mails, anything that looks dusty is an immediate turn-off. It says old-style and not of the minute.
- The verbose and flowery. The great advantage of e-mail is the bite-sized quality of it. Long-winded and pompous e-mails would fail any test.
- Slow. People expect a reply quickly. Any e-mail that takes a couple of days to arrive is too slow.
- Blunt or brusque. E-mails are an opportunity to be

appropriately personal. They are you to me. Me to you. If they feel rude or plain blunt then it's a wasted opportunity.

- Overslangy. Jive talk is a turn-off in business e-mails. It seems lacking in respect and often ridiculous.
- Passive. Say who's doing what to whom. The passive verb has no place in the e-mail.

CHAPTER 5

Forms of rightness

We all know that e-mails are only going to become more common; perhaps they will become the first business communication method of choice, *the* standard form of communication. This is pretty exciting. It's like journeying into an entirely new, undiscovered realm.

One of the defining features of this new realm is that there are very few rules and very little agreement on what makes things right. If you asked someone to explain the conventions of e-mail writing, they would probably either be lost for words, or simply say that there aren't any.

This may sound exciting for it means there is considerable scope for trailblazing. But it's also a problem, especially for businesses. Where one of the problems with ordinary letters is that they are fettered by too many conventions, with e-mails the problem is reversed. There aren't any conventions. People just don't know how to write them yet. There are, however, some communications rules that hold good whatever the medium. Two that are helpful are:

Write always with the reader in mind;

Less is frequently more.

When faced with the absence of rules, people

generally do one of two things. Either they stick rigidly to what they know. Or they experiment wildly, and end up doing basically whatever they want. Conformity or anarchy: people will always choose one or the other.

We can apply this to the present, rule-less situation with e-mails in which some people either: write the old standard letters, and send them via e-mail; whilst others lapse into total informality.

In our view, neither of these options appeals very much. Traditional letters seem totally out of place. No matter how conversational you make a letter, there are still those conventions of language and structure which just don't feel right in an e-mail. The letter pretending to be an e-mail always makes the sender look a bit dusty and the company it comes from unprepared for the challenges of the modern world.

But the alternative isn't much better. That kind of overdone, no-holds-barred informality. You know the stuff: 'Hi mate . . . check this out . . . catch you later.' Or even worse, geek-speak, all weird words and symbols that no one but a select crowd of in-geeks can understand. Fine for an e-chat between friends, maybe. But hardly the language in which representatives of a business should converse with customers. This approach just looks schoolboyish. It seems to show a lack of respect for the reader. Worse still it shows a clichéd and unimaginative response to the possibilities of the new medium.

Just because e-mails are new doesn't mean we should reach for the fake funky talk.

Modern business English has moved on tremendously in the last ten years. It has caught up with the trend towards a more egalitarian and accessible style in public and private life. Many of the so-called rules of grammar have been abandoned – thankfully. It's OK to start a sentence with 'and'. And 'but' is fine at the start too. It is common to see letters even from rather stuffy organizations that are more personal and spoken in style. Personal pronouns and contractions abound. All of this is good, because it begins to value writing as communication and not simply as either message-giving or evasion. It metaphorically takes the bowler hat off business language. We can now be sure of the following things:

- the dusty writing of the past does not signal that writing is businesslike;
- people of all walks of life and all income brackets prefer a more conversational, human writing style;
- people are far more marketing-literate and can sniff out the phoney and the overblown immediately;
- there is a premium on getting any messages over quickly because people have far less time and are far less patient.

Modern language has undoubtedly contributed to a more open, conversational environment at work. More accessible writing breaks down boundaries and bureaucracy. The contribution of pioneering groups like the Plain English Commission has been immense. But so too has the general movement to a more brand-aware environment that puts a premium on speaking in the customer's language and style and not the company's.

It is less acceptable to see jargon or bureaucratic writing, although some sectors have been slow to move on. Just ten years ago I would regularly be greeted with folded arms and stony silence when I suggested something as conventional as plain English as a language strategy for banks, building societies and the like. These days in boardrooms and meeting rooms across the world the response I get is quite different. The message is:

**Help us to write like real
people writing to real people.
Let's get rid of the old
ways of writing.**

These changes have played into the hands of e-mail, which is ideally suited to a more vernacular, more modern style. Indeed e-mail may have helped to drive the change towards more modern writing styles in the workplace.

The e-mail and the letter

But the e-mail and the business letter cannot be exactly the same. The e-letter also needs to be geared to the special requirements of electronic communication.

What are those requirements? And, more importantly, how can we go about using them to construct a novel, practical, dependable form for effective, on-key business communication?

Rules should never be completely inflexible. When they are, we are in danger of losing sight of their original purpose, which is to enhance communication. When rules become an end in themselves, language seems to freeze in its tracks. Over-regulation is the death of the word. But the current anarchy seems to be helping no one.

There is more than a crying need for guidelines, some broad principles. People need to understand what they're aiming for. Only then can they start making realistic choices about their cyber communications. Only then will they become masters of Net-iquette.

The new rule-book: e-style

In this section, we're really going to get down to the nitty-gritty of e-writing. We're going to look in detail at some concrete examples of e-mails, written for an imaginary business, Public Air. What makes them tick? In what way do they manage to steer that all-important middle course between stiff formality and total drop-out casualness?

But first we're going to, as they say, think big. So here are a few broad conceptual tips, before getting our hands dirty amidst the real hardcore cut-and-thrust of e-communication.

Five tips for tip-top e-mails

1 THINK AS IF YOU WERE SPEAKING. Whatever you do, don't put on your writing hat, or likely as not you'll end up with some stilted style that would look good in a museum. Try speaking a sentence in your head, or under your breath, to get the right combination of rhythm, fluency and warmth. It should have a sense of flow.

2 THINK CONVERSATION. You're engaged in a dialogue, an act of personal communication with someone, so your style should be that of a real person talking to another real person. Try to forget the technology between you. Your words should breathe personality and relationship.

3 THINK SIMPLE. As a writer you may be adept at knocking up dense, grammatically perfect sentences; in fact, you may rather like it. You may know how to join your modal auxiliaries to your main verbs, and your relative pronouns in subsidiary clauses to the subject. Or not. But the main thing is, don't forget your reader. The sentence you write is rarely the one that is read. To put it bluntly, it is usually uglier. So keep it short. Keep it straightforward. And keep it simple.

4 THINK CONCISE. Cut up convoluted snake-like sentences into shorter bites, and cut down windy paragraphs into cleaner, more airy blocks. But you don't need to leave out important information; concise means 'short in relation to what you need to impart'. This ties in perfectly with the e-mail medium. E-mails work because they are quick and bite-sized and dynamic. This is just what makes them a refreshing change from the business letter. So don't lose the advantage by overcomplication or having an attack of long-windedness.

5 THINK LESS FORMAL. But don't go over the top – employers don't want staff to start rapping to customers or treating them like old mates. Just remember that it's perfectly possible to be friendly and personal, as well as professional and expert. The key term here is less formal – less formal than the letter, more formal than the chat over the coffee machine. The perfect e-mail comes just about midway between these two extremes.

That's just to get your mind-set orientated for the more tricky task of looking at e-mails and considering the actual words themselves. Now let's get down to business.

With the traditional letter, signing on was never a problem. 'Dear Mr Smith' did very nicely indeed, thank you very much. But with e-mails, suddenly it's not so easy. Do we say 'dear' at all? And if we do, should it be capitalized? Doesn't this sound too much like the formal business letter? But if we dispensed with it would we upset the recipient. Would it sound too informal?

What about the name itself? First names are supposed to be OK in e-mails (so they say). But in truth it sounds pretty stupid addressing a client or customer you've never met before by their first name. Better keep the surname in, then, unless you're writing to someone you've either met personally or who you've already been in virtual communication with for some time.

But this only creates another problem. Do we now prefix the surname with a first name or initial, or do we return to the formal Mr/Mrs or Ms? As you can see, the varieties are endless, and there is little to guide us except intuition and common sense.

The trick, really, is to use your discretion. There is nothing wrong at all with writing out the name in full: 'Dear Sophie Hunter' – 'Dear David Webber'. It sounds polite, respectful, and also establishes a slight, but not overdone, level of intimacy with the reader. Avoid initials: they are best consigned to the antique fair. Titles – Mr, Mrs, Ms – are much preferable.

If in doubt, err on the side of formality. Stick to the good, honest title. After all, you might not know anything about the person you're writing to. And while no one is going to be offended by being addressed as a Mister or Missus, there are probably some people who would be a touch miffed if they weren't.

But there are variations. Sometimes a simple 'Hi' might be OK. It all depends how well you know the person and how well they know your business. It might not work for a bank. But it might very well work for an Internet-only bank!

Signing off is another problem area. The old 'Yours sincerely' really won't do at all. It just isn't right for e-mails. So we can drop the sincerely bit. But then 'Yours' on its own is overly familiar, only really suitable to someone you know pretty well.

So what are the alternatives? Here are a few:
Regards
Kind regards
Best regards/wishes
All the best
Wishing you well.
Of these, 'Regards' on its own is frankly a bit cold.

'All the best' is too familiar, while 'Wishing you well' is friendly, but not quite suited to a business context. Either 'Kind regards' or 'Best regards/wishes' manages to be courteous without being overformal or over-familiar. These are probably the best.

Then, all one has to do is sign one's name. Probably both fore and surnames. That way one can be personal, but at the same time keep the relationship on a professional footing. One of the dangers of any business e-mail is that it sounds too informal, too slangy and too presumptuous.

The one thing that is of paramount importance, though, is deciding on a format and sticking with it. This has to be a team effort. If a company's e-mails have a consistent look and feel, that immediately signals professionalism and attention to detail. The reader knows that a real effort has been made. He or she will appreciate it. We looked at this issue a bit further back in the section on writing on-brand.

But if e-mails are all over the shop, some starting like this, others like that, veering between formality and stiffness, then it will be clear that this is a company that hasn't given the matter any thought at all. And one that isn't tuned into the world of wired communication.

In order to look at some concrete examples, let's take a trip into fantasy land for a few minutes. We're now passing through the virtual lobby of that exciting new Internet company, PublicAir.com.

PublicAir is a company with a difference. They saw the problem with this issue of e-communication early, and took steps to deal with it. They gave their staff basic guidelines and some direction in brand identity and values. They asked them to write their e-mails in a consistent way – polite, courteous, responsive.

But above all, they gave them the freedom to express

themselves in their e-mails. The rules weren't laid down heavily like a set of commandments, because the bosses of PublicAir are themselves aware of one very important thing: People respond well to a bit of freedom and responsibility. Staff who are themselves respected will pass on that respect to the people they have to deal with.

Let's see how the people at PublicAir express that respect.

Example one: the info byte

> Dear Miss Johnson
> Many thanks for your e-mail.
> For information about our flight times, please visit our website – www.PublicAir.com. Simply go to the 'I want' box at the bottom right, and click on 'Flight info'.
> You should find answers to all your questions there. If not, don't hesitate to e-mail us again.
> Have an excellent trip.
> Kind regards
> <First name Surname>

What about that sign-on, 'Many thanks?' Well as we've seen, it's all a question of steering a fair course (as Odysseus said) between Scylla and Charybdis, between the painfully rigid and the laughably flaccid. 'We were most grateful to receive . . .' would be ridiculously formal, a mere 'Ta' would be too much the other way – so here we have an ideal middle course, warm and fulsome without being too chatty. It feels right for the e-mail medium and more importantly right for the company, which prides itself on being approachable and modern.

The point is that you need to take sensible decisions based on what your company is really like.

The theme of courtesy – saying please and thank you – is one that you should be able to trace through e-mails as much as conventional business letters.

Having begun with the 'thank you', this message continues with a 'please'. It directs the reader, simply and concisely, to just the part of the company website where she can access the key information. It gives the customer the level of help desired, with an offer of future availability if needed. Then we have the personal touches of:

'Have an excellent trip. Kind regards.'

Now this is not a study in stripped-down plain English; strictly speaking, no information is being given here. It's true that these words are excess to require-ments; they're purely and simply relationship-driven. And all the better for it, for the customer leaves feeling good about the contact she's had with PublicAir, feeling helped and feeling cared about. They have an air of easy informality. As a receiver of the e-mail you're likely to feel that these people are good to do business with. And notice how the humble e-mail is at the front line of developing and presenting the brand and the offer. The e-mail, done well, is the company represented in a little bubble of communication. Brilliant.

All in all, the ideal resolution and the perfect e-mail.

Example two: observational gratitude

Let's now take a look at a second example of good prac-tice, another e-mail sent out by PublicAir. This time it's in response to a customer who has written with a hand-ful of concerns and observations.

The customer has no specific complaint, just an interest in passing on some views. It's what happens in a relationship. When someone offers a comment or response or even criticism, the mature listener says: 'OK, I see what you mean' or 'Yes, that's true. I'll watch out for it in future' or 'Thanks, I'll try not to do that again.'

So the key here is to thank the customer for his time and efforts, and assure him that you – the entire company, as far as he's concerned – have paid serious attention to her. You acknowledge him personally, and you have noted his views. You also aim to use e-mail to its best advantage as a quick, warm human response. Much better in truth than the traditional letter at dealing with this kind of thing.

Dear Jonathan Hill
Thank you for your e-mail. We're always keen to have views and comments from our passengers – it's a vitally important way of improving and developing our services. So we're grateful you took the trouble to contact us and we'll certainly take into account what you say.
Thanks again.
Kind regards
<First name Surname>

This illustrates just the kind of tone we're looking for: simple, spoken, concise, courteous, relationship-centred. It's also personal and warm without being sickly, wet or offhand. The business e-mail after all represents a real physical organization (albeit on the Internet), a professional organization, and should come across accordingly.

So the tone of 'We're always keen . . .' and 'it's vitally important . . .' and . . . 'improving and developing our services' all reinforce the professional attitude of a company that respects its customers and is open to comments – and indeed welcomes such feedback as an essential part of improving overall service.

Finally, the all-important acknowledging line: 'we'll certainly take into account what you say' underlines and completes the customer contact. It also imbues the individual details of the interaction with an uncanny and miraculous ingredient X that renders the message greater than the sum of its parts. Consumer research repeatedly shows that this abstract feeling is what most customers remember, long after they've forgotten the particularities of a company's response. They remember that they were listened to by someone in this huge organization.

And the e-mail makes the most of itself as an e-mail. It is to the point. It has the feel of real fingers on real keyboards. It brings across the values of the brand strongly. It feels like real communication done in a modern way. Importantly, it doesn't feel like a letter that just types on to the screen. There is an e-mailness about it.

Example three: making the most of things going wrong
PublicAir.com is a great company. It has a fresh vision, offers excellent service, has a strong sense of brand personality and a corporate culture which prohibits inertia and allows creativity and initiative to blossom.

And yet . . . things will still go wrong. It may not happen very often, but as sure as anything, it will happen at some point. That's what life is like. You can't get away from the fact that people and machines go wrong, no matter how carefully you train (or programme) them, no matter how clever (or expensive) they are.

Any company worth its salt will realize this. That doesn't mean that failure will be expected, or that success won't be an overriding goal. It just means that the company will realize, like any mature adult, that occasional failure is par for the course. It isn't something which needs to be dreaded, or run away from. It just happens, and like anything which 'just happens', it needs to be accepted and dealt with.

But hang on a moment . . . is that quite right? 'Accepted . . . dealt with'. What do these words actually tell us? Take a closer look.

Well, they definitely indicate a certain maturity. Acceptance, after all, is a grown-up attitude, the mark of a well-rounded, balanced individual. The ability to accept and deal with things that aren't wholly desirable, that don't go according to plan, is a necessary precondition of coping with the unpredictabilities of life.

And yet, is acceptance quite enough? If we probe beneath this term, isn't there a somewhat passive attitude underlying it? It reminds us of that American car sticker, which solemnly proclaims that 'shit happens'. Well, true. It certainly does. You can't argue with this as a statement of fact. But the point, surely, is not that shit happens. It's what you (and 'you' here can stand for a company as much as an individual) go on and do with it. After all, simply accepting that shit happens doesn't stop you being damaged or crushed when it does. What's needed, in addition to acceptance, is something which prevents acceptance turning into passivity and resignation.

Take a glance through history, at all the examples of really successful people, and you won't find much to recommend the sentiment expressed on that car sticker. History is full of things going wrong, of unbearable suffering, of conditions of adversity. But what marks out the people who emerge from all that deprivation as truly successful is that they have taken the bad, accepted it (we'll concede that much) and have then gone on and used that adversity as the basis for something positive.

To return to our example, let's imagine something going wrong for this otherwise successful business. PublicAir is a transport company, and we all know what tends to go wrong in that business: the transport doesn't work.

In this case, pilot illness is the problem. Following a short-haul flight to Spain, two of PublicAir's pilots contract a serious stomach bug and are unable to make the return journey. Being resourceful, the company has reciprocal arrangements with other airlines, so that cover is provided in such situations. But unfortunately, because of other flight commitments, the cover takes a while to arrive, resulting in a delay of two hours to the flight.

The first thing PublicAir does is make regular announcements over the loudspeaker system, apologizing for the delay and keeping passengers informed on progress. When it becomes clear that this is going to be a serious delay, it sets up a desk where passengers can pick up $20 vouchers, to spend at the airport duty-free. It's not much in comparison to the overall cost of the flight ticket, but it creates an impression of genuine concern, and allows customers to indulge themselves in a small way while waiting for their flight.

All the signs are that the small token of goodwill has had the right effect. PublicAir receives remarkably few complaints about the delayed flight. One customer, however, is genuinely upset. In her e-mail, she explains that, as a result of the delay, she missed a connecting train and was consequently late for a family funeral. Not only is she upset, she's also angry. She wants to know why there isn't better cover for pilot illness. Surely a two-hour delay on a short-haul flight is far too long?

PublicAir has a small team of people responsible for dealing with the customer relations aspect of flight delay. To be honest they don't have all that much to do, because PublicAir does so much to create an impression of concern for its customers. Few customers feel the need to make further complaints afterwards.

However, when that does happen, the team is more than prepared. For them, writing e-mails in response to complaints is not something to be dreaded. Rather, it is an opportunity to re-establish the trust in a relationship which has been temporarily broken. What's more, they know that once this trust is re-established, the relationship will actually be stronger than it ever was before.

Let's see how they do it.

Dear Mrs Steadman

Thank you very much for your email. On behalf of everyone at PublicAir, I'd like to say at once that we are all very sorry about the delay to your flight. We realise how distressing it must have been for you to arrive late for such an important event. You have the fullest sympathy of everyone working here.

I'd like to take this opportunity just to explain how your flight came to be delayed. As the announcement made clear, one of the scheduled pilots fell ill shortly before the flight was due to leave.

When this happens, we are usually able to arrange for immediate cover with another airline flying from the same airport. On this occasion, though, I am afraid this wasn't possible. The large volume of air traffic around this time of year, combined with delays to other flights, meant that there was an unusual shortage of pilots that day. Our staff did their very best to book an alternative, but unfortunately this did take a while to arrange.

As a way of saying an extra sorry, we would like to offer you £50 off your next flight with PublicAir.

> Of course, this won't make up for your distress on your last journey. But we hope you can use it at some point in the future – hopefully on a much happier occasion!
> Best wishes
> [First name Surname>

Why is this e-mail so right for this particular customer? Let's look at a few of the main points.

- Like all PublicAir's communications, it's extremely courteous – 'thank you', 'sorry' and 'fullest sympathy' all crop up in the first paragraph.
- It offers a full, honest and clear explanation of exactly what went wrong. Nothing is hidden, there is no air of secrecy or sneakiness. It isn't too brief or abrupt. It shows it is possible to write a longer e-mail without waffling or becoming pompous. E-mails can be more than one paragraph long!
- There is nothing at all flippant or off-hand about the tone. The delay is treated as a very serious issue, with a real appreciation of the customer's distress.
- It reveals a strong and appealing sense of collective purpose and responsibility. The writer has the confidence to take it upon herself to apologize on behalf of others, without any sense of passing the buck or evading the issue. But at the same time, PublicAir does not come across as an inaccessible, impersonal corporate entity. Instead it is depicted as a team of responsible individuals, all working towards a single purpose. Hence, Mrs Steadman has the sympathy of 'everyone working here' rather than the remote condolences of 'our company'.

- The tone is personal, but in a respectful, not-too-chummy way. The writer has recognized that the passenger is upset, and with good reason, for she has missed a funeral. So the tone respects this – politely alluding to the funeral without actually saying something crass like 'I'm so sorry the flight was delayed and that you missed your funeral. It must have been very distressing for you'. That would have only reinforced the negative impression of PublicAir, whereas the tone that PublicAir has actually adopted will go a long way to regaining the trust and belief that here is a company which genuinely does take note of its customers' concerns.

Some big lessons
Grit your teeth, unclench yourself and have a go at this more spoken style next time you need to write a company e-mail to a customer or colleague. Be less businessy and more human. Get the feeling right and you'll hit the right note every time.

How low can you go?
One of the biggest debates about e-mail language is informality. Because the e-mail feels like such a new, exciting form, there is a big temptation to push back the boundaries of language, so to speak, and turn each letter into a work of experimental fiction.

We all know that risk is a good thing. And businesses need risk-takers. But when it comes to communication, businesses should leave artists to be the real trailblazers. You have to remember your customers. You can't necessarily expect everyone else to be as daring, or up-front as you might like them to be. There must be some sense of reserve – or else you're going to find people logging off your prose.

What you shouldn't do in an e-mail?

Don't
- use computer jargon
- use slang
- show anger
- swear
- write in the passive
- sound dry
- sound uninterested
- use computer geek jargon (emoticons etc.)

If you've read this chapter carefully, you should be in a position to write excellent, focused e-mails, the kind that will stand your business in good stead for the coming age.

Above all, don't get drunk with the excitement of it all – the new technology, dreams of a strange wonderful future where none of the previous rules apply.

If that is what you're looking for, then we're afraid the prognosis isn't so good. The Internet isn't quite such a break with the past as you might think. When it comes to written communication, the same basic rules still apply. Be warm, be open, be respectful, be fun.

In fact, the basic message is the same throughout this book, whether we're talking traditional letter, e-mails or mailshots. Sensitivity and attentiveness are paramount in all your writing. It's the basis of good customer relations, and that, after all, it the springboard to business success.

Writing check
To sum up if you can answer yes to all the following statements then you are likely to be writing as near perfect e-mails as possible.

1 My e-mails are personal and conversational.
2 I avoid waffle.
3 I write in a more modern accessible style.
4 I understand my company culture and brand and write my e-mails to reflect these things.
5 I try to step into the customer's shoes and write with them in mind.
6 I avoid jargon and a bureaucratic tone.
7 I keep things simple without becoming patronizing or brusque.
8 I'm not afraid to write with a sense of enjoyment and fun where appropriate.

And if you can answer no to all of these then you're even further forward.

1 I enjoy writing in a high-handed rather pompous style.
2 I believe the e-mail is just an ordinary business letter but sent by a different route.
3 I write what I want to without thinking of the receiver.
4 I write long sentences.
5 I am a fan of the passive verb.

Reality check
Two reasons why the net isn't changing all the rules:

- Technologies aren't exclusive. When something new comes along, it doesn't necessarily spell the end of what went before. People didn't stop writing letters when the phone was invented, did they?
- E-mails are only one way of communicating, they aren't the full story. Letters are still important and are likely to continue to be so. E-mails won't replace

letters but they will and have had an influence on them.

Two reasons why it is:

- Words are just going to get more important. After all, what is the Internet but a global bank of words, accessible to everyone. As we said earlier, e-mail has made the art of writing sexy and vital again. As WAP technology advances and the quick message is going to become more and more a part of our daily lives, words are going to speed up, becoming ever-more snappy and punchy.
- The Net gives everyone the chance to communicate, and be communicated with. Nowadays, no one can afford not to be a master of wired words. And everyone needs to keep on learning and looking for ways to rise to the challenges.

CHAPTER 6

Ready to go

ROUNDING UP

We do hope you now have a handle on the perfect e-mail. But just to sum up, here is a resumé of some of the main points we have raised.

A challenge – but also an opportunity
The single, overriding theme of this book has been the transformation of challenge into opportunity. We have seen how the e-mail raises all sorts of new and tough challenges and choices, for the individual and for businesses. Some of these are scary; others are bemusing. But the trick is not to shy away from difficulty. Rather, see it as an opportunity – for new experiences, new initiatives and, above all, new successes.

Changing with a changing world
As we saw earlier dealing with change is fundamental to human existence. Our ability to adapt is what marks us out from other species.

However, that doesn't mean we are always willing to embrace change. There are lots of reasons – psychological, organizational – why we want things to stay as they are. Coming to terms with the e-mail is about letting go of many of our old assumptions. Change needs to be seen not as a hostile terrain to be avoided at all costs, but as a fertile uninhabited territory just waiting to be colonized. Whatever the case, change is with us.

Communication at pace – don't be left behind!

E-mails are fast; as part of the Internet, they bring immediacy of access to the written word, where previously it was reserved for the spoken. This means that other things connected to the e-mail are also speeded up. Writing becomes faster, more punchy, to the point. Many of the formulas appropriate to the posted letter no longer have a place.

At the same time, expectations change. It doesn't take long to write an e-mail, and only a second to send one. So, a week's delay in responding to an e-mail – an acceptable amount of time for a letter – seems like a positive affront.

Companies must realize this. It is no longer possible to send a customer or client query around the various department inboxes, waiting for someone with a spare half hour to draft a response. Instead, everyone needs to be prepared to take immediate responsibility for sending e-mails. As roles become more flexible, so must the burden of responsibility.

From the management point of view, this means having enough faith in your employees to let them take that responsibility. It also means having just the right amount of control. From the staff point of view, it means being sufficiently motivated and committed to rise to the challenge of taking it.

Flexible communication – guided by a controlling hand

So, we know that one of the defining features of the

e-mail is speed, and that this means companies being prepared to place more trust in their employees.

But this raises other, organizational, issues. How is the standard of business communications to be maintained? How can companies ensure that their e-mails have a consistent content, feel and tone?

Remember, every e-mail is a little window on to the company brand. It needs to be more than a simple message, conveying information. It needs to present a snapshot of the world of that company. At its best, it should be capable of conjuring up a set images and associations in the reader's mind, drawing them into the company ethos and identity; personality should breathe through every word.

So what organizational steps should be taken to make this ideal a real possibility? In this book we've touched on some novel ideas – e-mail libraries, in-house style and tone guides and classes.

But perhaps most important of all is not to be too dictatorial. Remember that the Net is a democratizing force, stripping away many of the old hierarchies and practices. One effect is that a brand identity is, in the last resort, no longer an abstract, manufactured thing, externally created and imposed from the top down. Rather it is a living, breathing entity, expressing the combined personalities of all the people working for a particular company.

So, the message for managers is:
- get the right people working for you;
- impart to them your aims and aspirations – what you stand for and what you believe in;
- share with them your vision and, even more importantly, let them contribute to it;
- invite them in and give them the space and freedom

to become a part of your collective personality, not simply a representative of it but an essential, creative agent within it;

- let them express and contribute to that personality through their communications and, in particular, through writing the kind of e-mails that send out the message 'We are a company with assurance and confidence. We value our customers because they help make us what we are. We are living, breathing organization, made up of living, breathing people who will treat you – the customer – not like figures on a computer screen but as living, breathing people also.'

If you do this you will craft modern e-mails that are genuine and do reach out to customers. And the perfect e-mail? Perhaps it hasn't yet been written; after all it is early days. But certainly the more perfect e-mail will be all of the following:

1 human
2 personal but not too personal or presumptuous
3 bite-sized
4 more conversation without being conversation itself
5 full of the right level of flavour.

The future
So we hope you're ready to go. But before you do, why not stay with us for a moment to take a small glimpse into the future world of e-mails.

Because, **This is just the start of the story.**

We are truly at the beginning of the e-mail revolution. E-mails are still quite new, although growing quickly in popularity. As with any change, we'll all get more used to them and find new and ingenious ways of making the most of the new technology and the opportunities it presents. The e-mail books of the future will take for granted many of the ideas that feel new here. Whatever happens, we hope that e-mails will become more on-brand, more successful, and that their wonderful spontaneity and intimacy won't be sacrificed to the peril of standardization.

In twenty years there will be newer and quicker ways of communicating. This is bound to happen. We will live in a wireless world. The mobile will be king – or its children will. The e-mail may be dead. We may communicate simply by the power of thought. We may all routinely be using video conferencing on our mobiles. Who knows, we may be beaming ourselves around the world! The e-mail may have become just one aspect of e-communication rather than the whole of it. We may routinely be sending sounds and pictures down the line.

But whatever happens we can be sure that we'll need to continue to develop the way we write.

Two factors we can predict.

- Speed. Change is not going to get any slower. This means there will continue to be a premium on getting messages across quickly and effectively. E-mails have started this trend. In today's world we need to write in bite-sized chunks, something e-mails prepare us for perfectly.
- Promiscuity. Customers will get even more picky and demanding. They will demand writing that feels right to them. So tone of voice is likely to become more and more important. Get the tone wrong and they will leave and go somewhere else. Get it right and they might just stick with you for a little longer. Just might.

Also Available

THE PERFECT PRESENTATION

Andrew Leigh and Michael Maynard

Many people are terrified of making a presentation in public, while others are just unsure of how to go about it effectively. But the ability to do it successfully can make all the difference to your personal career, and to the business prospects of your firm. This book provides a sure-fire method based on the 5 Ps of Perfect Presentation: Preparation, Purpose, Presence, Passion and Personality. It is an excellent, hands-on guide which takes the reader step by step to success in one of the most important business skills.

£6.99   0 09 941002 8

THE PERFECT NEGOTIATION

Gavin Kennedy

The ability to negotiate effectively is a vital skill required in business and everyday situations.

Whether you are negotiating over a business deal, a pay rise, a difference of opinion between managers and staff, or the price of a new house or car, this invaluable book, written by one of Europe's leading experts in negotiation, will help you to get a better deal every time, and avoid costly mistakes.

£6.99   0 09 941016 8

PERFECT TIME MANAGEMENT

Edward Johns

Managing your time effectively means adding value to everything you do. This book will help you to master the techniques and skills essential to grasping control of your time and your life.

If you can cut down the time you spend meeting people, talking on the phone, writing and reading business papers and answering subordinates' questions, you can use the time saved for creative work and the really important elements of your job. Learn how to deal with interruptions, manage the cost and cut down on meetings time – above all, how to minimize paperwork. You'll be amazed how following a few simple guidelines will improve the quality of both your working life and your leisure time.

£6.99   0 09 941004 4

THE PERFECT BUSINESS PLAN

Ron Johnson

A really professional business plan is crucial to success. This book provides a planning framework and shows you how to complete it for your own business in 100 easy to follow stages.

Business planning will help you to make better decisions today, taking into account as many of the relevant factors as possible. A carefully prepared business plan is essential to the people who will put money into the business, to those who will lend it money, and above all to the people who carry out its day to day management.

£6.99   0 09 941005 2

PERFECT ASSERTIVENESS

Jan Ferguson

Perfect Assertiveness helps you to understand more about assertiveness and its importance as a life skill. The book shows you the difference between assertiveness and aggression, and teaches you to understand more about yourself, the possibilities of change and the potential for improvement in personal, social, family and workplace relationships.

£6.99   0 09 940617 9